Lonely No Longer

Mark A. Finley

R. A. Williams Library
Florida Hospital College of Health Science
671 Winyah Drive
Orlando, FL 32803

Hart Research Center
Fallbrook, California

Unless otherwise indicated, all Scripture references in this book are from the New King James Version of the Bible, copyright © 1972, 1984 by Thomas Nelson, Inc.

Edited by Ken McFarland
Cover art direction and design by Ed Guthero
Cover illustration by Darrel Tank

Copyright © 1993 by Hart Research Center
Printed in the United States of America
All Rights Reserved

The author assumes full responsibility for the accuracy of all facts, references, and quotations as cited in this book.

ISBN 1-878046-35-7
BV 4501.2 .F56

Contents

    Before You Turn This Page v
1. He Is on Our Side 7
2. In Good Hands 17
3. Without a Doubt 35
4. When Accusing Voices Are Silenced 45
5. More Than Skin and Bones 57
6. Lonely No Longer 71

Before You Turn This Page . . .

This little volume is filled with incredibly good news. Each page pulsates with hope and encouragement. After criss-crossing continents conducting evangelistic meetings for the last decade in some of the world's major cities, I have become convinced that many people need the inspiring message these pages offer.

Does discouragement settle in on your life like a dense fog? At times do you doubt whether your sins are forgiven? Are you filled with guilt over the past? Do you seriously wonder whether you will be saved? Do you feel insecure, uneasy, and troubled? Do you struggle with thoughts of low self-esteem? Do you feel no one understands you?

All of us are plagued with doubts sometimes. We all struggle with our own insecurities and basic fears. But there are eternal truths which we need to be reminded of again and again. This book can make a significant difference in your life. It can open new doors of understanding. It can revolutionize your concept of God and your understanding of who you are in His sight.

As you thoughtfully read these pages, you will discover a God who loves you more than you can possibly imagine—One who already has forgiven you before you ask; One who reaches out to you before you reach out to Him; One who values you beyond imagination; One who completely understands and is always there.

As you read these pages, pause often to meditate on the beauty of what you are reading. Internalize the concepts set forth here. Praise God that as you confess your sins, you do indeed receive His forgiveness. Accept the fact that you are His son or daughter. Enjoy the privileges which are yours in Christ, for in His daily loving presence, you will be *lonely no longer*.

1

He Is on Our Side

Many years ago, an ordinary factory worker saved up enough money to go on a luxury cruise. It took all of his savings to purchase the ticket. Anxiously, he awaited the date of his departure.

Since he had used his savings for the ticket, he realized he could not afford to eat in the ship's expensive dining hall. So just before departure, he purchased some cheese and crackers in a little inexpensive grocery market.

The first few days of the cruise, things went well. He enjoyed the magnificent ocean views, marveled at the brilliant sunsets, and relaxed by the ship's swimming pool. But he was definitely tiring of cheese and crackers . . . crackers and cheese. The aromas wafting from the exquisite dining hall, along with the comments of other passengers regarding the delicious meals, enticed him. He could stand it no longer.

With cautious hesitancy, he inquired of the chief steward, "Sir, how much are the meals?"

"May I see your ticket, please?" the steward asked. Examining the ticket, the steward replied in surprise, "Didn't anyone tell you the meals are part of the package? They come with the ticket!"

The poor man was living below his privileges. This story may be true or fictional—I am not particularly concerned with that. What does concern me is that in the Christian life, this sort of thing happens all the time. Countless Christians feel guilty, insecure, and fearful. They lack any assurance that one day they will live forever in heaven with Christ. They wonder whether God really answers their prayers. They have difficulty dealing with temptation. They feel an obvious lack of spiritual power. They are uncertain in knowing how to discover God's will for their lives. They are desperately frightened when they consider the judgment.

In this chapter, we will focus on our security in Christ. We will consider the great certainties of the Christian life. "That you may know the certainty of those things in which you were instructed." Luke 1:4.

Our sense of security and assurance as Christians grows as we make such discoveries as the following:

- ■ Knowing our sins are forgiven

- ■ Sensing that God accepts us

- ■ Valuing ourselves as God values us

- Coping with temptation
- Knowing God's will

What is your concept of God? Is He for you—or against you? Is He your ally—or your enemy? Is the way of eternal life so hard that only a few spiritual giants can be saved—or has God made it easy to be saved and difficult to be lost?

I remember, as a boy, hearing the Christmas song about Santa Claus that talked about his "making a list and checking it twice," and that "he knows if you've been naughty or nice." The naughty ones, of course, got no toys at all. So we were all on our best behavior (for at least one day before Christmas anyway!).

Is God some kind of cosmic Santa Claus, checking His list "twice" to see if you've been "naughty or nice"? Does He check His master computer list daily to find out if you have sinned? To you, is God a strict, austere judge? Nothing could be farther from the truth! What *is* true is that God has taken the initiative in our salvation! He has a pre-designed, personalized plan to save us.

Before you ever were born, God developed a plan to save you. "For whom He foreknew, He also predestined to be conformed to the image of His Son . . . Moreover whom He predestined, these He also called." Romans 8:29, 30.

A Personalized Plan

Taking into account your genetic make-up, your personality traits, your early childhood influences, and the impact of both your heredity and environment, the

Master Strategist developed a personalized plan to win you to Himself. "Before I formed you in the womb I knew you." Jeremiah 1:5. See also Isaiah 43:1, 7; 49:1, 2. "For there is no partiality with God." Romans 2:11.

Throughout your entire life, God has been seeking you. He has enlisted all the agencies of heaven to save you:

Jesus. According to John 1:9, Jesus is the light of truth, who illuminates the mind of each man or woman born into the world. He is the inner light, guiding the conscience and working through the mind to lead each individual to right and truth. He places within each person a sense of "rightness" and "wrongness." This is precisely why even primitive cultures have a sense of morality. Repeated disobedience certainly violates this inner pull toward righteousness. Cultural practices contrary to God's will may squelch it. Nevertheless, innately—at birth—it is there. God Himself places it within every human being as a powerful agency to draw us to Himself. He is doing everything He can to save us.

The Holy Spirit. According to Romans 2:4, through the Holy Spirit, God continually impresses our minds of His goodness, to lead us to repentance. Before we turn to Him, He appeals to us. And through the Spirit, God convicts us of right and wrong.

The Angels. Hebrews 1:14 asks: "Are they not all ministering spirits sent forth to minister for those who will inherit salvation?" Angels wing their way from worlds afar, enabling us to understand truth. They cooperate in mysterious ways in drawing our minds to Jesus.

Divine Providence. God is continually arranging circumstances in our lives to draw us to Himself. At times He brings us miraculously into contact with other people who are Christians. A piece of literature, an inspiring book, a radio or television program, all may play a part in nudging us toward the kingdom. At times He mercifully allows difficulties to occur in our lives to develop a sense of need within us. Sickness, marital or family problems, financial setbacks, or difficulties at work or school—any of these might be wake-up calls from a loving heavenly Father.

The all-powerful agencies of heaven are working for your salvation. God is on your side. He has taken the initiative. He has set in motion a plan to save you. And He has enlisted every divine resource possible to effect your salvation. However interested you may be in seeking God, He is far more interested in seeking you.

Consider Adam's rebellion in the Garden of Eden. After sinning, Adam hid from God. Filled with guilt, he certainly wasn't seeking God. His fear of punishment led him to run.

In loving concern, God took the initiative. God sought him out. God reached out to him. In words of tenderest love, our gracious heavenly Father called to Adam, "Where are you?" Genesis 3:9. What an incredibly loving God we have!

When we first moved to England, my wife and I found driving on the "left hand" side of the road difficult. And the first few times out on the road, the English round-abouts nearly scared us to death.

Getting up her courage, my wife drove alone to

Watford one day a few years ago, just before Christmas. The streets were absolutely packed with Christmas shoppers. Our son Mark, who was about seven at the time, got lost. My wife panicked. For fifteen minutes she searched, calling frantically. Quickly, she organized groups of passers-by to form a search party.

Who was putting more effort into the search—my wife, or my boy? Did she idly say, "Look, son, you pulled your hand out of mine. You wandered away from me. You are lost, and I hope you find your way back. If you do, fine. If you don't, that's your problem"? Not at all! Nothing else mattered except finding our son.

God not only has a pre-designed plan to save us, He has taken the initiative in carrying out that plan. He calls us to Himself.

God is like that. Romans 8:30 joyfully proclaims the good news: "Moreover whom He predestined, these He also called." Not only has God pre-designed a plan to save you, He actively calls you to accept that plan.

God is the Good Shepherd who, at great expense to Himself, wanders through the night seeking the one lost sheep (see Luke 15).

God is the Good Samaritan who comes seeking us as we lie bruised and bleeding on the highway of life. He cradles us in His arms, whispers encouragement in our ears, and at infinite expense to Himself, takes us to the inn of safety (see Luke 10).

God Takes the Initiative

Yes, God is a seeking God. In Christ, He has taken

the initiative. In Christ, He left the splendor and glory of heaven and entered this snakepit of a sinful world to redeem us. In Christ, He left the worship, adoration, and praise of the angels. He left the joy of heaven—the companionship of cherubim and seraphim.

We may resist that love. We may reject it. But we cannot avoid it. We cannot run away from God's love. Around every corner, we come face to face with Him. He is there calling, wooing, entreating, appealing tenderly.

David found God's pursuing love overwhelming and described it in Psalm 139:5-18:

Verse 5—"You have hedged me behind and before."

Verse 6—"Such knowledge is too wonderful for me."

Verse 7—"Where can I go from Your Spirit?"

Verse 8—"If I ascend into heaven, You are there; if I make my bed in hell, behold, You are there."

Verse 17—"How precious also are Your thoughts to me, O God! How great is the sum of them."

Verse 18—"If I should count them, they would be more in number than the sand; When I awake, I am still with You."

The poet Francis Thompson called God "The Hound of Heaven." Constantly pursuing, constantly seeking, constantly taking the initiative. Like a young man in love, He is the aggressive one. We don't chase Him; He is chasing us.

"We Can't Get Away!"

A few years ago, I was conducting an evangelistic series in a Holiday Inn in Brockton, Massachusetts. One evening after preaching a sermon on "How to Discover Bible Truth," I extended an invitation for people who desired to accept Jesus, follow truth, and look forward to baptism, to come forward. Among others, a young woman in her late twenties responded. Slowly, her story unfolded.

This was her first night at our meetings. She had earlier learned about the Bible while living in Canada. She had studied with an Adventist pastor, had accepted Jesus, and was attending church while preparing for baptism.

Her husband became very upset. In an attempt to get away from these new truths his wife had embraced, he suggested a short vacation outside of Boston. His plan was for them to attend his brother's wedding and then spend a few days relaxing.

Reaching Brockton, they attempted to find a room at several other motels, only to find them all booked. Finally, they found a room available at the Holiday Inn.

After checking in, they discovered that our meetings were in progress there.

"We can't get away!" the husband exclaimed. "We have run right into this Bible business again!"

It is true that you can't get away from God. You meet Him around every one of life's corners. You bump into Him in life's dark spots. He is always there—seeking you, reaching out to you, tapping you on the shoulder, whispering in your ear, prompting your conscience.

As Adam and Eve, Jonah, and so many others through history have found, you can't get away from God. He is committed to saving you! And even if you aren't running away from Him—even if you desire Him—He desires you more. Yet the intensity of your desire for Him is no accurate measure of His desire for you.

Your desire for Him may be weak. His desire for you is strong. Your commitment to Him may be on today and off tomorrow. His commitment to you is constant. Your grasp on His hand may be slipping. But His grasp on yours is firm. Your love for Him may be shallow. But His love for you is deep.

God longs to save you. He has a pre-designed plan to win you back. Daily, He calls you. You can be secure in a love like that. For God has taken the initiative. He is on your side. And that makes all the difference!

2

In Good Hands

Dr. William P. Wilson, professor of psychiatry at Duke University, is a world-renowned specialist in his field. His articles on psychotherapy have been published in major clinical journals. Both the American and British psychiatric societies—as well as other specialists in the medical community—have carefully reviewed his work.

At the age of forty-four, he sensed that something was missing in his life. This sense of "emptiness" led him on a spiritual journey resulting in his conversion to Christ.

As a committed Christian, Dr. Wilson has attracted further world-wide attention by applying biblical insights to the field of psychotherapy. His clients often feel a need for acceptance, love, security, and joy in their lives. In his book *The Grace to Grow*, he tells the story of Peter.

Peter was born with a severe visual impairment. Even with his half-inch-thick glasses, he could only make out shadows. As a child, he never learned to read. Constantly teased at school, he soon dropped out. His mother resisted all of his father's attempts to discipline him.

Soon he became a pampered and spoiled child. Throwing temper tantrums to get his own way, he learned that almost anything he wanted could be his if he yelled loudly enough.

At ten, he began stealing inexpensive items out of small stores. By twenty-one, he was a compulsive thief. Stealing gave him a sense of satisfaction—a sense of power, of being in control. By thirty, his garage was filled with items from hardware stores from all over town. Although he did not use the items and kept them in their original packaging, he kept stealing.

Attempting to carefully analyze Peter's problem, Dr. Wilson worked to bolster his self esteem by sharing scriptural insights. Within a year, Peter had developed an entirely new self concept. Courageously, he returned the items he had stolen. He began to read a large-print Bible. Miraculous, unaccountable changes took place in his life.

At a Christian retreat for doctors, lawyers, and selected government workers, half-literate Peter shared the testimony of God's grace in his own life. Holding his large-print Bible six inches from his face, he began to read the reassuring message of Ephesians: "Having predestined us to adoption as sons by Jesus Christ to Himself, according to the good pleasure of His will, to the praise of the glory of His grace, by which He has made us accepted in the Beloved." Ephesians 1:5, 6.

The spiritual insights in Paul's letter to the Ephesians changed Peter's life. They made a difference for him, and they can make a difference for you. Notice the highlights of Ephesians 1:3-10 and 17:

Verse 3—God has blessed us with every spiritual blessing in Christ.

Verse 4—He chose us before the foundation of the world. (Even before He made the world, He chose us to be His very own—*The Living Bible.*)

Verse 5—He predestined us to be His sons. (Such was His will and pleasure—*The New English Bible.*)

Verse 6—He has made us accepted in the Beloved.

Verses 7, 8—We have redemption through His blood . . . the forgiveness of our sins . . . the riches of His grace.

Verse 9—He makes known to us the mystery of His will—He shares with us His hidden purpose.

Verse 10—God gathers together all things in Christ.

Verse 17—God gives us the spirit of wisdom and revelation in the knowledge of Him. "I pray you will understand who Christ is and all that He has done for you" (*TLB*). "I pray God will give you the spiritual insight to know more of Him" (*Phillips*).

These concepts made a significant difference in Peter's life. They can make just as great a difference in yours! They are not dry, stale, boring religious concepts to be debated by university theology teachers. They are dynamic, biblical principles which give spiritual stability to life. Let's examine these principles a little more closely.

Principle number 1: In Christ, we have a new identity!

In Christ, each of us has **a new identity**—a new self concept. We are, in fact, members of God's immediate household—members of His family. Even before we were born, God chose us to be His children.

God has a pre-arranged plan to save me! Though I am wretched and lost in sin, a new identity is mine through Jesus! As I trust Him, I become His child. Ephesians 1:4 emphatically declares: "He [God] chose us in Him [Christ] before the foundation of the world." Verse 5 affirms that He has predestined us to be adopted as His children.

Paul declares that God's pre-designed plan is that, through Christ, each of us is to become a child of God. Before the world began, God's plan was that each created being relate to Him as a son or a daughter. All of the privileges of sonship were Adam's; Eve was to be a daughter of the King of the Universe. All the privileges of being children of the King are now ours. Adam was given "dominion" over the planet. This earth was given to him as a gift from a loving Father. In a sense, it was his inheritance. Through rebellion, Adam and Eve lost their inheritance. But through Jesus, the inheritance was restored.

The concept of adoption as God's children is a central theme in Ephesians and throughout the New Testament:

In Ephesians 2:19, we are declared to be "No longer strangers and foreigners, but fellow citizens with the saints and members of the household of God."

In Ephesians 5:1, the apostle states, "Be followers of God as dear children."

And 1 John 3:1, 2 gives us this assurance: "Behold what manner of love the Father has bestowed on us, that we should be called children of God! . . . Beloved, now we are children of God."

This question, "Who am I?" resounds in the heart and mind of every human being. It is especially relevant to the young. Every generation of young people embraces its own dress and hair styles, its own fads, its own way of speaking. All these are statements to the world that shout, "I am somebody!"

Children mimic their TV, movie, or sports heroes, assuming for the moment the identity of someone they consider famous or important. The message of their role-playing is clear: "Look at me! I'm somebody important!"

We never outgrow our need to establish a personal identity. Even as adults, we seek to define ourselves by what we do or what we own. "See who I am!" we say to the world. "See what I have!"

In Christ, each of us has a new identity. No longer are we defined by how we dress, what we do, or what we own. Instead, our identity is firmly rooted in our relationship to the King of the Universe. We are His sons and daughters!

This relieves us of seeking to create a personal identity through accumulating things, accomplishing things, or wearing things. Our identity is found in our relationship to God. He is our Father. Jesus Christ is our Brother. Nothing can change that. The frantic and doomed search to prove to the world that we matter is over.

In addition, because of our new identity in Christ, our past no longer defines our life's true history. No matter what our life has been since we were born, in the mind of God, our past actually began long before our birth. Ages before we drew our first breath, God predestined us to be His children. Through Christ, we have been adopted into the royal family of the universe. Unless we refuse to accept it, all the privileges of royal family membership are ours.

Alex Haley, a black American, spent more than a decade tracing his roots on three continents. He patched together bits and pieces of his family history as passed down through the centuries by word of mouth, census records, and family wills.

In time, he discovered that in the year 1767, his great grandfather had been kidnapped on the Gambia river in Africa and transported on a British slave ship, the

Lord Segonia, to Annapolis, Maryland. In 1768, his great grandfather was sold to John Waler of Richmond, Virginia.

Alex Haley's story of his search for his "roots" sent millions of others on an intense search for their own identity. Genealogical study has become exceedingly popular.

What are my roots? What are yours? Even Haley's "roots" go deeper than his research revealed. Through Jesus, the late Mr. Haley was not just the great grandson of a slave—he was a son of God.

In practical terms, what does being a son or a daughter of God mean in our lives?

For one thing, it means that we may abandon all our efforts to impress others with our looks, our money, our clothes, our position, or our achievements. We are far more important and valuable than any of these things could ever make us. We are sons and daughters of the most important Person in the entire universe!

It also means that we may abandon all of our feelings of inadequacy and inferiority because of our past. Our value and importance are not based on any good things we have done, and they are not diminished by any bad things we have done—no matter how bad they may be. Our value and importance are based on the fact that we belong to the royal family of the universe. Our Father is the King of everything!

Principle number 2: In Christ, we have a new security!

Our security comes from knowing that He has provided both freedom from guilt and power for victory. He is working in our behalf. Angels descend from the throne of grace, and the Holy Spirit ministers to our hearts. He arranges circumstances in our life. Our security is totally in what God provides.

"He has made us accepted in the Beloved. In Him, we have redemption through His blood, the forgiveness of sins, according to the riches of His grace." Ephesians 1:6, 7.

As sons or daughters of God, the Father offers us mercy and forgiveness through the blood of Christ. Even if we stumble in our attempts to serve Him, we are still accepted as His children. He does not cast us off when we fail. Not only does He freely forgive us, He openly accepts us. It is this forgiveness and acceptance which motivate our good behavior.

But, some may ask, isn't there a danger of becoming *too secure* in Christ? Isn't it possible that some will conclude that God will accept and save them no matter what—so therefore they are free to live as they please? Can too much security take away the incentive for Christian growth?

One thing is certain: We are not likely to grow as Christians when we *have no security* in Christ! And if we realize what our security is based on, we are not likely to take that security as a license to plunge headlong into sin.

Any individual who uses God's grace as license to sin does not understand grace. Coming to Christ, charmed by His love, accepting His unmerited mercy, receiving His gracious forgiveness, sensing we are His children, our affections are His. His love breaks our hardened hearts. It leads to repentance. Secure in His grace as

His sons and daughters, we desire to please Him. Realizing what He has done for us, duty becomes a delight and sacrifice a pleasure.

He grants us new hearts (see Ezekiel 36:26). He promises to write the principles of His law in both our hearts and minds (see Hebrews 8:10) as well as to give us His Spirit as power to obey (see John 3:5, 6). We now long to please Him. The chief desire of our lives is to do His will, as His desire was to do the Father's will (see Matthew 26:39; John 8:29).

Where Our Security Is Found

Our security in Christ is not based on our performance or behavior. We don't gain security through doing good things. If our security is based on our works, we will be constantly wondering whether we have ever done enough. We will be always asking, "At what stage am I secure?" Our security comes from what Christ has done for us—the life He lived; the death He died.

And once we realize and accept our security in Christ, He helps us to grow in Him as well. As we surrender our will to Him, He begins in us the work of developing a Christ-like character. And what He begins, He finishes! He is the "author and finisher of our faith." Hebrews 12:2.

Suppose I am in the first grade at elementary school. Some students, like me, are in the first grade. Some are in the eighth grade. Each student in the school has different learning abilities and problem-solving skills. But if we faithfully accept and do the lessons the teacher assigns, in time, we will graduate. Likewise, if

I faithfully accept the lessons my heavenly Father assigns me, I will grow in knowledge and character. He will see to it that I "graduate."

A Nazarene preacher once stated it pretty well when he said, "You're 'once saved, always saved,' IF you *stay saved.*"

My son is just as much my son when he makes mistakes as when he doesn't. Of course, he can choose to separate himself from the family. He has the perfect right to change his name. He is free to leave home at any time. Unless he acts rashly and chooses to sever his relationship with the family, he will always remain my son. He has the assurance that I will not angrily throw him out of the home simply because he has failed.

God does not cast off Christians who desire to live the Christian life when they fail. When in my imperfection I lose my temper and become angry, am I still a son of God? Let me ask a couple of questions. Your response will reveal whether you fully understand the gospel or whether you are trusting your own works for salvation and are insecure inside.

1. Let's suppose a Christian loses his temper. In his anger, he jumps into his car and smashes into another car head-on before he has a chance to repent and confess his sin. Is he saved or lost?

2. Are Christians saved when they do good things, but lost when they do bad things? Is it possible to be in God's grace—under His approval—one moment and out of His grace the next?

I think an evil thought—oh, I am out of God's grace! I confess (now I'm back in grace). I lose my temper (out of grace). I confess (in grace). I think selfish thoughts (out of grace). Saved . . . lost . . . saved . . . lost.

Qualified By Failure

When we fail, God leads us to deep repentance and sorrow. But failure does not make us less dear to the heart of God. Failure does not disqualify us for God's grace—it is our very failure that *qualifies* us for His grace! God's grace is *reserved* for fail-ers, for sinners, for those of us who are weak. The perfect angels of heaven who have never sinned and fallen don't need God's forgiveness.

One of my favorite authors once wrote these encouraging words:

> If in our ignorance we make missteps, the Saviour does not forsake us. . . . Satan may come to you with the cruel suggestion. "Yours is a hopeless case, you are irredeemable." But there is hope for you in Christ. . . . When sin struggles for the mastery in the heart, when guilt oppresses the soul and burdens the conscience, when unbelief clouds the mind, remember that Christ's grace is sufficient to subdue sin and banish the darkness. Entering into communion with the Saviour we enter the region of peace.—*The Ministry of Healing*, pp. 249, 250.

Let's suppose you are sleeping one evening. As is your practice, you put your wallet on the nightstand before going to sleep. Sometime during the night, your son tiptoes quietly into your room. Cautiously, he opens your wallet and takes out $20.00—enough for the remote control car his heart is set on. You wake up but say nothing. You are heartbroken to think your son would steal from you.

The next day, you call your attorney and arrange to put your son up for adoption, right? If he steals, that's it—he's out!

Of course not!

We don't kick our children out of the house when they fall and fail. We don't divorce our spouse every time we think he or she has done something wrong. Why do we so readily assume God rejects us when we fall short? Can He possibly be less patient and long-suffering with us than we are with our own flesh and blood?

Nonetheless, it is possible for us—through long and repeated rebellion—to sever our parent/child relationship with God. If we abuse and neglect and presume upon that relationship long enough, we will no longer care about it. The problem with open rebellion against God is that it hardens our hearts. We become less capable of responding to the relentless appeals of His Spirit. We shut Him out of our lives. It is perilous to persist in any course of action which knowingly takes us out of God's will. To reject His love makes us less capable of receiving it and leads us to the place where our spiritual faculties are blunted and we no longer care. Though God's fatherly love will never, EVER let us go, we can choose to let Him go—to shut the door on Him.

Principle number 3: In Christ, we have new possibilities!

In Christ, we have the promise of **new possibilities** (see Ephesians 1:13, 14). We have access to all the divine power of Christ as He resides in us through the Holy Spirit.

I once counseled with a young man caught in the grasp of moral failure. "I need more than forgiveness," he said. "I want to be free. How do you turn back bodily urges?"

As we remain in Christ, all things are possible through Him. For we are not left to struggle alone with impossible, ingrained urges to sin. The hereditary and cultivated tendencies to sin are not as strong as is His power to turn them back (see 1 Corinthians 10:13). Left to ourselves, victory is impossible. But not for Him. Just look at how many Bible characters overcame "impossible" character defects:

Peter overcomes his temper, Simon his hypocrisy, Matthew his greed, Mary Magdalene her adultery, James and John their ambition—each as they seize the promise of new possibilities through abiding in Christ.

Principle number 4: In Christ, a new destiny is ours!

In Christ, we have **a new destiny** (see Ephesians 1:10, 21, 22). This world is not our permanent home. In Christ, our eyes are fixed on a world yet to come. God's ultimate plan is to save me eternally in His kingdom. He will never be satisfied until I dwell eternally with Him.

> Having made known to us the mystery of His will, according to His good pleasure which He purposed in Himself, that in the dispensation of the fullness of the times He might gather together in one all things in Christ, both which are in heaven and which are on earth—in Him, in whom also we have obtained an inheritance.—Ephesians 1:9-11.

> This was His purpose: When the time is ripe, He will gather us all together from wherever we are in heaven or on earth, to be with Him in Christ forever.—Ephesians 1:10, *The Living Bible*.

This world has an ultimate, final destiny. Atheistic historian Andre Maurois once lamented, "The universe is indifferent. Who created it? Why are we here on this puny mud heap spinning in infinite space? I have not the slightest idea, and I am quite convinced no one has the least idea."

Maurois is dead wrong!

Paul knew where this world was heading—and so can you! There is an ultimate destiny for this world—and that destiny is heaven!

Bob Harrington is known as "The Chaplain of Bourbon Street." One day the New Orleans street preacher was walking down that very street. A bartender recognized him and questioned, "Where are you going, Brother Bob?" His quick response: "Heaven. I'm just passing through town."

The Hope of Heaven

When Corrie ten Boom's sister, Betsy, died a horrible death in a Nazi concentration camp, Corrie tried to hold on to the last tangible link with her sister—an old threadbare jumper. When she finally gave up the jumper, she wrote: "And so I left behind the last physical tie. It was just as well, for now what tied me to Betsy was the hope of heaven."

The choking tears of death subside with the promise of eternal life; the gnawing fears of unknown destiny are erased by the positive assurance of a future reward.

Peter's Last Wish

Some time ago, I performed one of the saddest, yet most joyful funerals of my life. I met Peter (not the same Peter mentioned earlier in this chapter) in Gdansk, Poland. His mother was a committed Christian and prayed for her son throughout his life. When I visited Gdansk to hold an evangelistic series in the Lenin Theater in 1987, the boy's mom pleaded, "Pastor, pray for my boy."

A few weeks later I learned that Peter had brain cancer. The only human solution was an operation. The physicians shaved his head, operated, and removed the tumor. But they didn't get all of it. The tumor grew. Radiation treatments seemed to have little effect. Peter had a second operation. Now his head was terribly scarred. The cancer continued to spread. His body grew weaker by the day.

Through the pain and suffering of it all, Peter began listening to my taped series of Bible lectures. The Holy Spirit convicted him. He opened his heart to Jesus, longing to be free from the suffering and agony of his life. The hope of heaven became real. He sensed that he was a son of God.

Peter urged his mother to get his rock records and break them. He told her where he had been hiding sensual magazines and asked her to destroy them. He had become involved in some of the occult arts. Again, he instructed his mother to destroy his occult symbols.

In a few months, he had lost sixty pounds. During the last two weeks of his life, he didn't eat and was down to eighty-four pounds. He vomited continuously.

On a cool Polish October morning, his mother called the church and asked me to come immediately. Peter was dying. I knelt before him, the basin in my hands, catching the vomit. His skin was yellow. His eyes rolled around in his head. His very breath smelled of death. Yet Peter's dying wish was for me to baptize him.

I clearly explained that it would be impossible to baptize him by immersion in his condition. I couldn't take him to the church—he was too weak. And a lake or river was totally out of the question. I gave him the assurance that Christ accepted him. Still, he continued urging me to baptize him. It was his final wish—his last request. He wanted the sense that all of his sins were washed away.

My heart was touched. I encouraged his mother to fill the bathtub with warm water. Peter stripped to the waist. I took him in my arms and carried him to the bathroom. We knelt there on the floor as I prayed. The presence of God surrounded us. It was one of those eternal moments in life in which I felt as if I could reach out and touch God—as if, should I open my eyes, I would see His face.

After prayer, I lowered Peter into the bathtub, into the watery grave of baptism. As I lifted him out of the tub, a smile spread over his face as he said, "I am Christ's. Eternity is before me, and death no longer frightens me, because my destiny is heaven."

Our loving Lord allowed Peter to live peacefully for another month, and then he closed his eyes in that sleep which will end when our Lord awakens him on the resurrection day.

In his final days, Peter fixed his eyes on a whole new

destiny. That new destiny led him to completely reorder his priorities. The same thing will happen to any one of us who "hitch our wagon" to the star of a whole new destiny in Christ. The things that were important before will seem irrelevant. The things that seemed irrelevant before will now seem supremely important.

What stupendous blessings are ours in Christ! In Him, we have a new **identity**, a new **security**, new **possibilities**, and a new **destiny**. Hollywood can't offer that! Nor can all the promises of Madison Avenue, all the money on Wall Street, all the pablum of New Age gurus and psychics, all the world's Christless religions, all the "insights" of psychotherapy, all the positive thinking and self-improvement tapes ever recorded, and all the glitz and fame and wealth the devil can dangle before us.

Why spend frustrating decades on this wretched planet in a fruitless search in all the wrong places for self-identity, for love, for acceptance, for self-realization, for your ultimate destiny?

Look up, my friend! In Christ, all this is *already yours!*

3

Without a Doubt

It was as if someone had thrown a cosmic switch and suddenly turned off the stars. Black clouds hid them from view. A breeze, gentle at first, swelled to gale force and lashed the waves into fury. The violent storm burst upon the sea suddenly. The disciples' small boat tossed like a cork at the will of the waves. These strong men of the sea were powerless to bring it under control. Wearily, they gave themselves up for lost. Hope danced away like a shadow. Like grains of sand, it slipped through their fingers. In the fierceness of the storm, alone in the darkness, the sea taught them their own helplessness.

Then they saw Him—walking on the water, His form illuminated. Was it Jesus? Or could it be a phantom forecasting their doom? But then He spoke: "Be of good cheer! It is I; do not be afraid." Matthew 14:27. No other voice was as comforting as His. In the midst of their despair, Jesus' encouraging words, "Be of good cheer," calmed their fears. In their anguish, He invited them to "not be afraid." Recognizing His voice, a peace filled their hearts.

Many, in their Christian lives, are like these disciples. Filled with fear and doubt regarding their salvation, they toil with all their might, striving to make it to the other shore. Daily, they battle the waves of uncertainty. Just as these disciples were worried about their physical lives, so thousands of Christians are insecure regarding their eternal life.

I've talked to scores in my evangelistic campaigns around the world who have expressed their insecurity in such words as: "I feel there is little hope for me. I'd like to be saved. But I probably won't be. I just can't seem to live the Christian life. I hope the Lord will have mercy on me. Yet deep down inside I feel plagued with uncertainty regarding my own personal salvation." Their experience is aptly described in the following story.

Carrying Our Own Burdens

One day a missionary working among primitive peoples was driving a large truck down a country road. He stopped and picked up a number of nationals who were carrying large baskets on their heads. As they proceeded on their journey, the missionary observed that even a few miles down the road, they still had the baskets on their heads. Stopping the truck in the middle of the road, he asked, "Why don't you put those heavy burdens down and rest awhile as you ride?"

"Oh, no!" they responded. "You have done enough. The least we can do is carry our own burdens!"

Many Christians carry a heavy burden of insecurity regarding their own salvation. They have doubts concerning their acceptance with God. Jesus' discussion with Peter that stormy night provides insight into solving the dilemma. Let's listen in on that discussion. "And Peter answered Him and said, 'Lord, if it is You, command me to come to You on the water.' So He said, 'Come.'" Matthew 14:28.

Jesus gently invites you and me to come to Him today as well. He reassuringly declares, "Come to Me, all you who labor and are heavy laden, and I will give you rest." Matthew 11:28. He adds, "The one who comes to Me I will by no means cast out." John 6:37. The final words in the Bible, in Revelation 22:17, encourage us: "And the Spirit and the bride say, 'Come!' And let him who hears say, 'Come!' And let him who thirsts come. And whoever desires, let him take the water of life freely." Come, come, come, is the invitation of our Lord.

Confidently, Peter ventures out of the boat upon the water. With a sense of pride, he triumphantly walks toward his Lord, looking back at his fellow disciples as if to arrogantly declare, "Look at me!" In self-satisfaction he trumpets, "Look at my accomplishments!" But the wind is strong. The waves are high. And he no longer sees his Saviour. Recognizing that on his own he is going down, that the cold waves are engulfing him, he is now filled with doubt. He believes that he's not going to make it. He senses that he's going to drown. He cries out, "Lord, help me!" And Jesus simply responds, "O you of little faith, why did you doubt?" Matthew 14:31.

We, too, can identify with Peter. At times we are doubting Christians. We doubt that our sins are forgiven. Guilt plagues us. We doubt that we are accepted by God. We feel insecure. We doubt that eternal life is ours. We feel afraid about the future. Jesus gives us assurance today, just as He gave Peter assurance back then. Satan insinuates doubts. The following comment places Peter's experience and ours in perspective:

> Satan is ready to steal away the blessed assurances of God. He desires to take away every glimmer of hope and ray of light from the soul. But you must not allow him to do this. Do not give ear to the tempter but say, "Jesus has died that I might live. He loves me and wills not that I should perish."—*Steps to Christ*, p. 53.

One of the great Christian hymns says, "Blessed assurance, Jesus is mine. O, what a foretaste of glory divine." The words of the hymn were written by Fanny Crosby, while the melody was written by Mrs. Joseph Knapp. Mrs. Knapp's husband was the president of one of the largest insurance corporations in America at the time—the American Metropolitan Life Insurance Company. One day Miss Crosby was invited to Mrs. Knapp's home to listen to a new melody that Mrs. Knapp had written. As the story goes, Mrs. Knapp was playing the melody and asked Miss Crosby what the melody suggested to her. Quick as a flash, Miss Crosby responded, "Mrs. Knapp, your husband deals in life insurance. My heavenly Father deals in assurance. This song says to me, "blessed assurance, Jesus is mine."

Your heavenly Father does deal in assurance. He wants you to have the assurance that your hand is in His—that your sins are forgiven, that you are a child of God, that all the power necessary to live the Christian life is yours. Doubt is destructive. It is one of Satan's greatest weapons.

Satan's Retirement Sale

In my imagination I picture an auction. Satan announces his retirement to his evil angels. To raise adequate retirement money, he decides to auction off the formulas for varying kinds of sinful behaviors. The time of the auction is announced.

Satan begins auctioning off his evil wares. The auction proceeds all morning and long into the afternoon. Satan shouts, "I have the formula for lying. What do you bid for it? Here is the special formula for dishonesty. What will you give me? Castles, palaces, country estates? When we overthrow the world and reign, what will you give me for the formula for greed or pride. What? Yes, what is your bid?"

Each formula to sin is stored in a special golden jar with a hazy, evil-looking mist around it. Soon all the jars are sold . . . except one. The evil angels shout, "You must sell that one too! We'll give our richest palaces in exchange for it."

"No," Satan replies. "This one formula is used for professed Christians. It works almost every time. When they are under it's spell, they have no defense against sin."

"At least tell us what it is," the evil angels persist.

"It is doubt," Satan responds. "This formula deceives Christians into doubting God's love, doubting they're His children, and doubting that salvation is possible. It's my most powerful weapon. I will never sell this formula, because if I can get Christians to live in a world of uncertainty and doubt, I can lead them to commit any other sin. When they lack assurance, they are vulnerable."

Satan repeatedly used this formula on Jesus in the wilderness. He would preface his challenges to Christ with, "*If* you are the Son of God . . ."

"Is it really true," he was implying, "that You are God's Son? Look at You, Jesus. You are haggard, worn, and hungry. Your emaciated form and filthy, ragged garments betray You. You certainly cannot be the Son of God."

Satan's strategy was to instill doubt. In Gethsemane and on the cross, he again attempted to insinuate doubt. His strategy was to separate the Son from His Father by leading Jesus to question His true identity as God's Son.

Is it possible to have a calm assurance that you are a child of God, accepted by the Father? Is it possible to know that your hand is in Christ's hands and that you are on the way to heaven? Is it possible to be certain that the gift of eternal life is yours right now?

The Scriptures make plain that it is possible to have this assurance. 1 John 5:12 says, "He who has the Son has life; he who does not have the Son of God does not have life." Accepting Jesus, we receive the living Christ into our hearts. He brings with Him the gift of eternal life.

Verse 13 adds, "These things I have written to you who believe in the name of the Son of God, that you may know that you have eternal life, and that you may continue to believe in the name of the Son of God." Accepting Christ, believing in His salvation, we receive the gift of eternal life. And according to the Scriptures, we can know that we have it. God wants us to live in confidence, not in fear and doubt.

My favorite author once wrote:

> The perishing sinner may say, "I am a lost sinner," but Christ came to seek and save the lost. He says, "I came not to call the righteous but sinners to repentance." Mark 2:17. I am a sinner, and He died upon Calvary's cross to save me. I need not remain a moment longer unsaved. He died and rose again for my justification, and He will save me now. I accept the forgiveness He has promised." . . . the Lord imputes unto the believer the righteousness of Christ and pronounces him righteous before the universe.—*Selected Messages*, book two, p. 392.

What precious thoughts!

In my hopelessness and despair, feeling the dark, ugly waters of life pulling me down, I can cry out to Jesus. Accepting His death on the cross in the place of my death, I can have the assurance that He "will save me now."

I see Him, in my mind's eye, presenting His righteousness on my behalf before the heavenly universe. I listen as He pronounces me righteous before the heavenly hosts. New hope fills my heart. New joy floods my soul. By faith I believe that Christ's death on Calvary was for me. By faith I accept His pardon. By faith I accept His righteousness in the place of my failures. By faith I accept His perfect obedience credited to my account. By faith I imagine Him bearing my guilt, suffering my pain, and experiencing my death. By faith I accept the fact that through His death I can live eternally. By faith I am His child. By faith I accept His offer of eternal life.

Coming to Jesus does not require severe mental effort or agony. It is making an intelligent choice to accept by faith the sacrifice of Christ on Calvary as my own. He died that I might live. When I make that fundamental decision, all the privileges of being a child of God are mine.

Look away from your fears. Look away from your doubts. Look away from your weakness. Look away from your sins. And believe that God loves you. In Christ He has pardoned you—you are His child.

Isaiah 45:22 says, "Look to Me, and be saved, all you ends of the earth! For I am God, and there is no other." Salvation is a matter of looking, of choosing, of deciding, of depending upon Jesus. It's a matter of faith in Him.

Believing—or faith—is an act of the will. We choose to respond to the Holy Spirit's prompting. We choose to receive Christ's pardon. We choose to accept His death on Calvary as our own death to sin's guilt and power.

Hebrews 12:1, 2 says, "Looking unto Jesus, the author and finisher of our faith." Where do we look? To Jesus. Not to our sins. Not to our weaknesses. Not to our frailties. But to Jesus. Where is our confidence?

In Him. Not in ourselves. Not in our abilities. Not in our good works. What are we saved by? His grace. Not our righteousness. In Him, we are secure. Through Him, we are pardoned. By Him, we are adopted as His children. Accept His promises by faith and say, "Blessed assurance, Jesus is mine."

4

When Accusing Voices Are Silenced

I think that we're going to be indebted to Peter through all eternity. Peter speaks for us all. There is something about his humanness that I really like. I can identify with his experience. You probably can too. Peter is no isolated saint, sitting in some monastery praying all day. In the rub of life, he speaks his mind. He frankly lets you know where he stands. At times, he is impulsive. On other occasions, he's outspoken. But he's always honest.

One day Peter came to Jesus and asked an important question. "Master, my brother sins against me. How often shall I forgive him?" Before waiting for Jesus' answer, in his characteristic way, Peter answered his own question: "Master, seven times?" (see Matthew 18:21). Peter thought this was some brilliant revelation. He assumed Jesus would applaud him for his willingness to forgive. He thought Jesus would send him to the head of the class of disciples.

Three Strikes, and Then . . .

The rabbis had a saying: "If a person sins against you once, forgive him. If he sins against you twice, forgive him. If he sins against you three times, forgive him. If he sins against you four times, repay him for his sin." They thought that three times was enough to forgive anybody. After that, mercy was exhausted. Justice then demanded retribution.

Rabbi Hanna, a famous Jewish rabbi of the first century, made this observation: "He who forgives his neighbor must not do so beyond three times." Rabbinical law required justice after the third offense. Here's a statement of another famous rabbi: "If a man commits one offense, forgive him. If he commits two offenses, forgive him. If he commits three offenses, forgive him. If he commits four offenses, do not forgive him."

The rabbis had the idea that God forgives three times, but that beyond three times, even God would punish. Peter thought that to forgive a brother seven times was akin to Godlike perfection. He took forgiveness far beyond the limited pharisaical idea. This is why he questioned, "If a man sins against me, shall I forgive him seven times?"

Seven is more than double the number of times the rabbis were willing to forgive. Seven is the number of perfection. Now can you understand why Peter expected Jesus to approve his statement. Peter thought Jesus was going to pat him on the shoulder and happily proclaim, "Peter, a marvelous truth has dawned upon your mind." Imagine Peter's surprise when Jesus said to him, "I do not say to you, up to seven times, but up to seventy times seven." Matthew 18:22. How much is seventy times seven? 490.

What was Jesus really saying to Peter? Do you recall in the prophecies of Daniel, where Jesus declared that He would give Israel 490 years of grace following their Babylonian captivity? After their continuous rebellion, God would accomplish in their captivity what it was not possible for Him to accomplish in their prosperity. Year after year, His mercy was extended to the Jews. In love, He sent them messenger after messenger. Then He sent Jesus, and they crucified Him. For 490 years He offered forgiveness, yet Israel continually rebelled. They rejected His repeated offers.

Forgiveness By the Numbers?

It was as if Christ were saying to Peter, "You talked to me about forgiving seven times, but My forgiveness cannot be measured in those limited terms. I have already reached out to Israel, the chosen people, for over 490 years. Peter, forgiveness cannot be measured by numbers. Forgiveness is an attitude of mercy toward those who have wronged you."

Would God ask Peter to have this attitude and not have it Himself? Forgiveness is rooted in God's nature. He is gracious and merciful. He holds no grudges. He harbors no resentments.

Three facts are essential to understand if we're going to experience the forgiveness that God desires us to have. These important principles are sometimes misunderstood by conscientious Christians.

First, forgiveness is rooted in the very heart of God. In Luke 15 we have one of the most beautiful interruptions in the entire Bible. The prodigal son comes to himself, senses his sin, prepares a memorized confession while still in the pigpen, and heads home.

But before he confesses, the father has already forgiven him. Forgiveness is rooted in the father's nature. The father runs to meet his wayward son. Immediately, the boy begins pouring out his prepared confession. But the father interrupts. Throwing his arms around his son, he assures him of his love. Placing a royal robe around his shoulders, he welcomes him home. The father does not stand aloof, waiting for the boy's confession, before giving him the assurance of his love. His attitude is one of forgiveness all along.

Opening the Floodgates

Forgiveness is not something we *earn* by confessing our sins. It is something we *receive* by confessing our sins. Our confession does not change God's attitude toward us. Rather, it enables us to appreciate God's attitude toward us. Our confession does not alter God's mind. The purpose of confession is not to plead with God to give us something that He doesn't long to give us already.

Forgiveness is rooted in the very essence of the character of God. His forgiveness is flowing out to us in the symbolism of the water of life that flows from the

When Accusing Voices Are Silenced 49

throne of God. Our lack of confession is like a dam that holds back the river of the water of life so it doesn't reach us. When we confess our sins, the floodgates open, and we receive the river of forgiveness flowing from God's heart all the time.

Some things are indivisible. To divide them is to alter their chemical composition. Air is a compound made of oxygen, nitrogen, argon, and carbon dioxide. To change any one of those chemicals—to leave out the oxygen, nitrogen, argon or carbon dioxide—is to change what air is. What remains would not be air. God would not be God if His forgiveness were earned by confession. It is rooted in His very nature as God.

Now notice the second beautiful truth. God provides forgiveness through Jesus independent of anything we do. It's easy for us to think that our prayers form the basis of our forgiveness. Yet forgiveness never rises from our prayers but from Christ's prayer. While wicked men were crucifying Him, Jesus prayed, "Father, forgive them, for they know not what they do."

The author of the world's best selling volume on the life of Christ wrote: "That prayer of Christ for His enemies embraced the world. It took in every sinner that ever lived or should live from the beginning of the world to the end of time."—*The Desire of Ages*, p. 745. Just as Christ forgave His enemies before they asked, so forgiveness flows from the heart of God before we ask. Did the Father answer Jesus' prayer on the cross? He certainly did. Calvary testifies to it.

Now, I do not mean that everyone accepts God's grace, but rather that it has been granted for all.

Likewise, not everyone accepts His forgiveness. But God has already forgiven the human race, independent of any human response. Heaven provides forgiveness through Christ, independent of any asking or endeavor on our part. Forgiveness is an accomplished fact. I do not earn forgiveness by confession. God's attitude toward me does not change when I confess.

If you had only five minutes to live, what would you do? Many Christians would quickly try to remember all their sins and confess them. Then they would ask for more time, because five minutes isn't long enough. This concept is based on a wrong assumption. It's rooted in the idea that if a committed Christian who has a growing relationship with Christ ever sins, he's lost. It is rooted in the idea that if I have any unconfessed acts or attitudes of sin in the slightest degree, then I am alienated from Christ.

The apostle Paul describes the relationship of the believing Christian to our Lord in these encouraging terms: "For as many as are led by the Spirit of God, these are sons of God. For you did not receive the spirit of bondage again to fear, but you received the Spirit of adoption by whom we cry out, 'Abba, Father.'" Romans 8:14, 15. When we become Christians, we are adopted into the family of God. We become children of God. The Father loves us as He loves His own Son. If one of my children fails, it does not imply rejection. And I'm certainly not a better parent than God. It's certainly reassuring to know that.

As one Christian classic puts it, "Even if we are overcome by the enemy, we are not cast off, not forsaken or rejected by God."—*Steps to Christ*, p. 64.

If a Christian sins and then dies before he verbalizes his confession, is he saved or lost? It all depends on his inner attitude of sensitivity to the Holy Spirit. If his attitude is one of conscious rebellion, yes, he's lost. If his inner attitude is one of repentance in response to the Spirit's promptings, he is still God's child and certainly not lost, even though he has not yet verbalized his confession.

Why Confession Is Important

Does this mean that confession of specific sins is unimportant? Not at all. This leads us to the third key point regarding confession and forgiveness. We must individually accept God's forgiveness before it effects our salvation. Confession is vitally important for at least two reasons. First, God respects my freedom of choice. Although He has provided forgiveness, He will never force it upon me. Although it's rooted in His nature, it cannot be received in my heart unless I choose to receive it. His forgiveness never works changes in me unless I desire it. It can never pardon my sins unless I personally embrace it. He respects my freedom of choice so much that the forgiveness rooted in His very nature will never become mine unless I ask for it.

Another reason confession is so important is that every act of disobedience, disloyalty, and rebellion reacts upon me. If I fail to recognize that my sin builds barriers between me and Christ, I will become spiritually hardened. Sin is not merely breaking a law, it's wounding Jesus. How many times can you continue to wound Jesus and still be sorrowful afterward? That's the real problem. Not that we'll ever exhaust His forgiveness—but that through our indifference and carelessness, through our failure to recognize the specific things we do that stand between us and Christ, we will come to the place where we become indifferent to the things of God and no longer want forgiveness. Our misdeeds, unless we constantly face them, will interpose a barrier between us and Christ. Sin hardens our hearts. Confession softens our hearts. It keeps our moral systems clean. Confession is important because it enables God to help us when we need it most. And it enables Him to minister healing to our hearts.

Martin Niemoller languished for months in one of Hitler's prisons. During his long imprisonment, he spent hours thinking about questions of life and death. He reevaluated his life. Quietly he prayed, "Lord, I cannot resist Your love any longer. I accept Your forgiveness. I believe I am Your child."

When Niemoller was released, he made this penetrating observation: "It took me a long time to learn that God is not the enemy of His enemies." Romans 5:8-11 outlines this truth marvelously. "But God demonstrates His own love toward us, in that while we were still sinners, Christ died for us. Much more then, having now been justified by His blood, we shall be saved from wrath through Him. For if when we were enemies we were reconciled to God through the death of His Son, much more, having been reconciled, we shall be saved by His life. And not only that, but we also rejoice in God through our Lord Jesus Christ, through whom we have now received the reconciliation."

The Incredible Trade

We are His enemies, but He is our friend. We deserve nails through our hands, but He took them and places instead a scepter in our hands. We deserve the crown of thorns, but He wore it so we can receive a crown of glory. We deserve the tattered, bloodstained robe, but He wore it so we can receive a robe of righteousness. He died the death that was ours so that we can live the life that was His. As a just Man, he was condemned so that we the unjust can be set free.

Before we ask, His attitude is one of forgiveness. Before we repent, His Spirit impresses us with sorrow for sin. Before we confess, His mercy surrounds us, creating within us a desire to repent. Why hide in a cave of doubt when you can stand in the sunlight of assurance? Why carry burdens of guilt when you can rejoice in His forgiveness?

In Stockholm, Sweden, one evening, I was visiting one of the city's travel agents. She had been coming to our meetings in the heart of the city. As we discussed spiritual things, she asked, "Pastor, I have a question I've always wanted to ask a minister. Is abortion murder?"

"Why do you ask?" I responded. "Do you know someone who has had an abortion—or are you pregnant and contemplating an abortion? Or might it be that you've asked because you're troubled that sometime in the past you personally had an abortion?"

With tears in her eyes, she blurted out a story of thwarted love, of an unwanted pregnancy, and of her hasty decision to abort her baby after carrying it for three months.

After her first marriage broke up, she met a man she believed was the man of her dreams. He was from another country. She fell in love. She dated him for six months. He promised to marry her. They talked about purchasing a home. During their engagement, he broke the news that he was already married and had three children in another country. He was convinced he now needed to leave and return to his family.

She was devastated. She felt used. Her first marriage had fallen apart, and now, with the collapse of her second relationship, she could not stand to bear a child by a man she had once thought she loved but now hated. Being pregnant out of wedlock, she decided on an abortion. She never felt comfortable with what she did. She was plagued by an inner restlessness, an inner sense of guilt, a sense that she had committed murder.

For eighteen years she bore the heavy, oppressive burden of that guilt. Gently, I explained that when Christ died on the cross and cried out, "Father, forgive them, for they know not what they do," that His forgiveness was for her. His forgiveness was there all the time. It was rooted in His very nature. Together we read 1 John 1:9: "If we confess our sins, He is faithful and just to forgive us our sins."

"Does the text say," I asked, "'If we confess our sins ... except abortion'?"

"Oh, no!" she responded.

"Would you like me to write in your Bible, 'If we confess our sins ... except abortion'?" I asked.

"Certainly not!" she added.

Tears filled her eyes. She began to realize that what

When Accusing Voices Are Silenced 55

God promises is really true. She grasped by faith His promise, "If we confess our sins, He is faithful and just to forgive us our sins." A new peace flooded her soul. Forgiveness had been available for eighteen long years, yet she only received its benefit when we knelt down and she confessed her sin, opening her heart to receive it.

Long ago, a woman of great spiritual insight wrote this of those who bear a burden of guilt unnecessarily:

> [They] do not really believe that Jesus pardons them personally and individually. They fail to take God at His word. Many who all their lives have walked under a cloud would be filled with amazement as they view the channels overflowing with mercy instead of dark clouds heavy with wrath and denunciations. They go about as under a weight of woe and condemnation when they might have peace and comfort and hope and fullness of joy.—Ellen White, *Review and Herald*, Sept. 21, 1886.

You can have peace and comfort and hope and fullness of joy. Reach out by faith to receive it. Accept what Christ has already wrought out for you on the cross.

In the late 1960s, American news focused on the returning Vietnam veterans. But there was another who was returning home as well. For twenty-five years he had hidden in the mountains of the Philippines. This Japanese World War II veteran, still clad in the ragged fragments of his uniform, was a frail, emaciated specimen of humanity. For twenty-five years he had lived in fear, not knowing that the war was over. Cut off from civilization, he had wandered through the jungles, barely surviving, living in fear and doubt.

When he was found, wandering around those Philippine jungles, it was hard to convince him that the war was over. He thought that this news was merely a deceptive ploy of the enemy.

Other imprisoned souls still live in dungeons of unbelief today, carrying huge burdens of guilt. But the war is over, friend. Jesus sets the captives free. You need no longer live in the dungeon of doubt. You need no longer battle with guilt. Forgiveness is yours for the asking. Reach out and receive it today.

5

More Than Skin and Bones

Clara Anderson was a maid in San Francisco. Clara was a very gentle woman—and very conscientious. One day after having worked for the same employer for fifteen years, she disappeared. Her employer had no idea where she had gone. She seemed to have just dropped out of sight. Then miraculously, after days of searching, the city's social services department found her.

Clara was in the process of starving herself to death in a mountain hideout outside of San Francisco. She said, "I want to die. Leave me alone." When the reporter who ultimately found her interviewed her,

Clara said, "Look, nobody cares about me. I'm just a maid—just one of thousands in society doing menial tasks. My life is of no value. I have no close relatives, no family, no friends. I'm so lonely that I don't want to live. There's no one I consider close to me—nobody I can talk to, nobody I can open my heart to. So just let me die, because nobody really cares."

Nobody Cares!

"Nobody cares!" is the desperate cry of men and women on a lonely planet. Someone has said that the disease of the nineties is depression, caused by low self-esteem. Some time ago *Newsweek* magazine ran a feature article called "Runaways" on teenagers who had left home and were now living in major cities throughout America. One seventeen-year-old was living in an old flophouse with no heat and poor food. Reporters asked her, "Why don't you go home? Your parents are upper middle class Americans living in a comfortable house. You could have good food, your own car, a nice room with a stereo, and luxury vacations with your parents! Why don't you go home?"

The girl responded, "Yes, I have everything, but I am worth nothing."

Ann Landers tells an interesting story in one of her columns. She describes a man outside a western city who waited for eleven hours after his car had broken down for somebody to stop and help him. It's an amazing commentary on human life. The man was just a few miles out of town when his car broke down. He stepped out of the car and attempted to flag down passers-by on the freeway who were traveling sixty or seventy miles per hour. Not one person stopped. It was a terribly cold night. Soon the weary traveler gave up hope. The suicide note he left on his car windshield read this way: "I have been waiting for eleven long hours for somebody to stop. I can't stand the cold any longer. They just keep passing me by." So he ended it all.

Clara and this man who committed suicide had something in common. They felt they were of little value to anyone else. They felt that no one really cared.

Russell Baker, a newspaper columnist, wrote an interesting homily describing his feelings about being one of four billion people on the face of Planet Earth. He summarized the despair of our times in a piece entitled "Nobody Knows Where."

> I'm sitting 93 million miles from the sun on a rounded rock which is spinning at the rate of a thousand miles an hour and roaring through space to nobody knows where, to keep a rendezvous with nobody knows what, for nobody knows why. And all around me whole continents are drifting aimlessly over the planet. I'm sitting here on this spinning, speeding rock surrounded by four billion people, eight planets, one awesome lot of galaxies, hydrogen bombs enough to kill me thirty times over, and mountains of handguns and frozen food, and I am being swept along in the whole galaxy's insane dash toward the far wall of the universe. And as I sit here, 93 million miles from the sun, I'm feeling absolutely miserable.

What a picture of twentieth-century men and women, crying out from the depths of their beings, "Nobody really cares!"

You may have heard of the contest held on a college campus to define the word *life*. The winning definition went this way: "Life is the penalty for the crime of being born." What despair! What hopelessness! Do human beings really have value? Are we simply skin covering bones? Are we merely enlarged protein molecules? The evolutionary hypothesis has given rise to a whole generation who feel that human beings are simply advanced species of the animal creation.

What Are We Worth?

Jesus gives us a totally different picture. He reveals God's estimate of human worth in that timeless story of the good shepherd. Once you understand God's estimate of human value, the illusionary myth of low self-worth is burst like a balloon in a carnival shooting range. In that magnificent story that Jesus Himself told, our true human value is graphically portrayed:

> So He spoke this parable to them, saying: "What man of you, having a hundred sheep, if he loses one of them, does not leave the ninety-nine in the wilderness, and go after the one which is lost until he finds it? And when he has found it, he lays it on his shoulders, rejoicing. And when he comes home, he calls together his friends and neighbors, saying to them, 'Rejoice with me, for I have found my sheep which was lost!'" Luke 15:3-6.

The eastern shepherd cares deeply about the sheep. He's willing to leave the comfort and convenience of home to traverse desert sands and to hasten through narrow, rocky ravines with blistered feet, bruised knees, and bloody hands to find the one lost sheep. He climbs over rocks, slides down steep crevices, and wanders through thorns and briars with one thing on his mind—finding the sheep which was lost.

George Adam Smith gives us this picture of the eastern shepherd:

> On some high moor across which at night the hyenas howl, when you meet him, sleepless, farsighted, weather beaten, arm leaning on his staff, looking out over his scattered sheep, every one of them on his heart, you understand why the Shepherd of Judah sprang to the front in the people's history.—William Barclay, *Luke*, p. 207.

This parable tells us three things about human nature. First, the shepherd was concerned about each individual sheep. Second, he carefully observed that one was missing. And finally, to the shepherd, the sheep were not merely part of a herd of animals. He noted each one individually. What a picture of God! No wonder God likens Himself to an eastern shepherd. As God looks at the human race, He doesn't see masses of humanity clawing at one another for living space. He sees individuals. Individuals who are precious in His sight. Individuals who are valuable. We are more than skin covering bones. We are the unique creation of God.

The prophet Isaiah encourages us with these words:

> For I am the Lord your God, the Holy One of Israel, your Savior . . . Since you were precious in My sight, you have been honored, and I have loved you. Isaiah 43:3, 4.

Precious, honorable, and loved! These are God's thoughts toward us. This is God's way of describing us. When the genes and chromosomes came together to form the unique biological structure of your personality, God threw away the pattern. There is nobody else like you in the universe. And for that reason you have immense value in the sight of God. You are precious. Some pieces of art by Michelangelo or Leonardo da Vinci are absolutely irreplaceable, because they are unique. There is no way God can replace you. You are unique in His sight.

You Are One of a Kind

I am told that when Swiss lace makers make their beautiful lace, they sometimes design their patterns from a single snowflake. Each snowflake has a different pattern. Since no two snowflakes are alike, no two patterns are alike. There is no one else like you in the universe. You are not merely a leaf floating in the autumn breeze. You're not merely a pebble on the side of the road, or a blade of grass. You are like that snowflake—individually created by God, one of a kind, special, unique. People cannot be reproduced on photocopy machines.

I once heard of a young lady who worked in an office all summer editing elementary-school textbooks. This necessitated her being away from her husband for a lengthy period of time. One day she got the bright idea that after work was over, she would send her beautiful face home to her husband via the photocopy machine. Cautiously, she lifted the top of the machine . . . smiled beautifully . . . closed her eyes, then placed the rubber covering that holds down the paper on the back of her head and pushed the button. As she pushed, the machine jammed, and an alarm went off. A repairman had to be called.

You just cannot photocopy an individual. People

cannot be mass produced like plastic spoons or knives or forks. They are not knocked out on a machine in some factory. You and I are uniquely created by God. There is no one else like us in the universe.

As you read these lines, you may be thinking, "It's good that there's nobody else like me in the universe. I'm glad of that. The world couldn't take another one of me." But think about it. If there were somebody else just like you in the universe, your worth would be reduced by at least 50 percent. As we look at the parable of the good shepherd pursuing one lost sheep, it clearly reveals God's view of human nature. The individual is important.

With billions of people on earth clawing at one another for living space, it's possible to wonder, "Does God even know I exist?" I certainly have asked myself that question. What difference does it make whether I serve Him or not?

Let's suppose that a lady had ten children. One of those children—a seven-year-old boy—is out playing baseball on the front lawn. His older brother hits the ball out into the street. While the young tyke is running after it, a driver speeding down the street at fifty miles an hour hits his brakes too late. He skids and hits the boy, killing him.

As a pastor, I'm called to have the funeral for the child. Wondering how I might help the mother, I come up with what I believe to be a brilliant idea. To help her overcome her grief, I decide to discuss all the advantages of the boy's death. Placing my hand upon her shoulder, I say, "Mother, I'm really sorry for what's happened to your boy. I know that it must bring you grief. And as I've thought about it, I've thought about how I might encourage you. I understand that you have ten children, true? Well, now, this means you only have nine left, right? And with only nine, you'll have more money and more time with less effort.

"You see, Mom, we have only three children in our family—two daughters and a son. My wife and I have had our hands full through the years with those three. I was just estimating that you're now going to have 10 percent more time to rest, 10 percent more money, 10 percent more dessert to go around, 10 percent more of everything. Think of what that child cost you in time and energy. Think of how much of your resources were dedicated to that child. Think of the positive benefits of his death. In fact, if you get a little lonely, you have nine other children to keep you company."

But all of her other nine children would not make up for her little Joey who had died. She would say, "No one smiles like Joey. No one hugs me like Joey. No one throws his arms around me like Joey and says, 'Mama, mama.' I don't want just anybody—I want one special somebody. It's Joey I miss. It's Joey my heart longs for. It's Joey's chair at the table that is empty."

If a mother has ten, does she love each of them any less than if she has only three? How many does a mother's heart have the capacity to love? One? Two? Twenty? Who put that capacity to love in the mother's heart? A loving God. And the same loving God who placed it in a mother's heart to love ten, seven, six, three, or one has an infinite capacity to love.

An Empty Place at the Table

One day a long table will be extended from one end of heaven to the other. Writing in the Bible's last book, Revelation, the apostle John calls this the marriage supper of the Lamb (see Revelation 19:1-3). Christ will serve each of us. He has set your place at the table. His loving eyes look down that long family table, and He's looking for you. If your place is empty, there will be an emptiness in His heart forever. If you are not there, you will be missed. You are unique. You are one of a kind. Your praise to Him ascends through the channel of your uniqueness—your specialness.

There is something God does not have unless you give it to Him—and that's your love. If you do not give Him your individual heart's affections, refined in the uniqueness of your personality, He will not have them. He will miss you forever.

The apostle John adds in Revelation 3:20: "Behold, I stand at the door and knock. If anyone hears My voice and opens the door, I will come in to him and dine with him, and he with Me."

The Love Hunger of Jesus

Suppose I were standing at the door of your house knocking. Would you invite me in? Would you? You say, Yes. If I am standing at the door of your house knocking and you invite me in and it's supper time, who provides supper? You do, of course. Where is Jesus as pictured in this text? Knocking at the door. Who opens the door? We do. We invite Jesus in for supper. And He is nurtured and nourished by our love. "Our Saviour thirsts for recognition. He hungers for the love and sympathy of those He has died to save."—*The Desire of Ages*, p. 191.

You can feed Jesus. You can nurture Jesus. You can satisfy His inner heart hunger for your love. In Luke 15, the individual shepherd knew each sheep personally.

Eastern shepherds would at times commingle their flocks. Two or three or four of these flocks would be mixed together. When it was time to bring the flocks back to the village, the individual shepherd called his sheep by name. These two or three hundred sheep, which were all mixed up, each recognized the voice of their individual shepherd and began following him home. Each sheep was known to its shepherd by name. If one was missing, the shepherd called the individual name of his sheep.

I love the way the book *The Desire of Ages* puts it,

> However large the flock, the shepherd knows every sheep. Every one has its name and responds to its name at the shepherd's call. As an earthly shepherd knows his sheep, so does the divine Shepherd know His flock that are scattered throughout the world. . . . Jesus knows us individually and is touched with the feeling of our infirmities. He knows us all by name.—*The Desire of Ages*, p. 479.

I would like you to notice carefully the shepherd's attitude toward his sheep. He knew it individually. As far as the shepherd was concerned, the individual sheep was his—he possessed it. When you and I come to Christ, realizing that we have immense worth in His sight, that He created us individually, we become His.

We are His sons and daughters. We're part of the royal family of heaven—related to the King of the Universe. And all the privileges of the family are ours.

Has this glorious fact dawned upon your consciousness yet? Has the marvelous truth that you are Christ's filled your mind? You are His by creation. He made you; He fashioned you; He has given you life. And you are His by redemption. You are purchased by His blood. You are not merely one of billions of people clawing at one another for living space in the universe. You have royal blood running through your veins. The individual sheep was possessed by the shepherd, and you become the possession of Jesus Christ. You are His. He cares for you. He loves you as if you were the only one in the world.

As far as the shepherd was concerned, the sheep was valuable enough to risk his life for. If the shepherd didn't return with the sheep, tradition says that at least he had to come back with the sheep's skin to indicate his willingness to fight off the bear or lion that had attacked the sheep.

Abandoned By God?

I would like you to picture Jesus in your mind right now with His hands outstretched. Imagine the cruel, rusty, blunted nails that are driven through that tender flesh. Imagine the nerves and tendons stretched out tightly on the cross. Imagine the fiery pain that shoots up His arms and the backs of His legs as He is suspended between heaven and earth. Imagine the crown of thorns jammed upon His head and the thick blood spurting from His temples and running down his beard. Look into His eyes filled with agony. Listen to His cry of woe. Hear His statements of grief. Feel the pain that shoots through His whole body.

Yet His physical suffering, painful as it was, constitutes only a fraction of His real suffering. The world's guilt which He bears shuts Him out from His loving heavenly Father. He is judged as a sinner—forsaken and accused. On the cross, He is alone. He feels His very soul being torn apart. Separated from His Father, He hangs in agony. Why does He suffer so? He experiences the pain that sinners will feel at the end of time when totally separated from God. With weeping and gnashing of teeth and intense wailing, they experience the agonies of hell, knowing that they will never be in the Father's presence again.

At this dark moment, Jesus does not see Himself coming through the portals of the tomb. He sees only the blackness of the grave and the horrors of death. But He is willing to experience it all for you and me. Calvary shouts to us, "You are valuable! You are mine by creation. I have made you. I have fashioned you. You are mine by redemption. You are more than skin covering bones."

The immensity of God's love is revealed on Calvary. I like the way the poet puts it:

> *Souls of men, why will you scatter*
> *like a crowd of frightened sheep?*
> *Foolish hearts, why will you wander*
> *from a love so true and deep?*
> *Was there ever kinder shepherd*

More Than Skin and Bones

half so gentle, half so sweet?
As the Saviour who would come
and gather us round His feet?
For the love of God is broader
Than the measure of man's mind.
And the heart of the Eternal
Is wonderfully kind.

Today, remember that you are something in His sight. Today, remember that you are more than skin covering bones. To God, your value is immense. You are one of a kind. You have unlimited potential. There is no one else like you in the universe. If you are lost, there will be an emptiness in His heart forever. If you are not saved, no one else can take your place. Heaven will be poorer because you are not there.

Friend, would you like to say something like this to Jesus today? "I want to be there. Lord, if you love me that much, no temptation on earth is as strong as that love. I give you my deepest heart's affections right now, and forever."

6

Lonely No Longer

Have you ever felt utterly, completely alone? As if you'd been cut off totally from human companionship? Loneliness afflicts a lot of us as we make our tiny footprints in the sands of time.

Even when there's a whole ocean of people around us, real companionship seems to come up, then slip away, never quite touching us—always just out of reach.

Recently, a sociologist at the University of Massachusetts conducted a survey of a cross section of Americans. Based on that, he estimated that as much as a quarter of the population feel extremely lonely at some time during any given month. That's fifty or sixty million people.

The problem is so pervasive it's produced a billion-dollar "loneliness industry." Video-dating clubs, special health spas, self-help books, all have sprung up to help people deal with their isolation.

Now admittedly, some of our loneliness is healthy and normal: "Situational loneliness," as the psychologists call it. That is our response to the breakup of a romance, moving to a new town, or the death of a loved one. We feel lonely and down for a while—and then usually, get over it.

But then there's chronic loneliness. Some people don't get over it. Some people seem to be lonely no matter what their circumstances. They have a hard time making social contacts. And when they do, they have an even harder time achieving intimacy. Loneliness can be a very miserable state of being.

Shy, introverted people are more likely to be lonely. The question is, What can they do about it? Are we all supposed to "quantum leap" into another personality, becoming jovial, talkative extroverts? Well, even if that were possible, it would probably produce more noise than companionship.

The truth is, we're pretty much stuck with our basic personality. But here's the good news: We *can* express our personality in better ways. We can use the tools we have in better ways.

A Starting Point for Overcoming Loneliness

Let's take someone who's shy and introverted, for example. There's a way in which that shyness, that pensiveness, can become a strength. Most of the people who communicated with God best—who were closest to God—were probably considered rather withdrawn by their peers.

What this means for lonely people is this: If you're having trouble communicating with people, the best place to start remedying that is by communicating with God. Why? Because God is so close to you—closer than you can imagine.

He is as close as a breath of fresh air in the morning, as close as the brilliant sunshine on a field of flowers, as close as a chirping robin or a gurgling brook. Nature, up close, suggests to us that the Creator's touch lingers in His creation.

Calling Heaven Is Not Long Distance

Listen to what the apostle Paul told some skeptical Greek philosphers in Athens. Acts 17:27, 28 says: "He [God] is not far from each one of us; for in Him we live and move and have our being."

Have you felt that God is rather remote—up there somewhere, rather than down here, right here? Well, please listen to this. The infinite, almighty God of the Bible presents Himself to us as a close Companion—as a very present help in trouble.

The Bible affirms that Jehovah is very near to all who call on Him. Listen to His wonderful words of assurance, spoken through the prophet Isaiah: "Fear not, for I am with you; be not dismayed, for I am your God. I will strengthen you, yes, I will help you, I will uphold you with My righteous right hand." Isaiah 41:10.

Don't be afraid, God says—you're not alone. I'm there to strengthen you—I'm close beside you. God comes into the closet with the one praying. He's at our right hand to support us. Human beings, Scripture says, can walk in the light of the divine countenance—we can behold God's beauty in the temple.

God isn't just some nice substance spread around everywhere. He is a Person, right here, knocking on the door of our hearts.

Let me tell you about one woman who felt terribly isolated and alone. Her name was Hagar. She served as an Egyptian maidservant in Abraham's household.

Abraham had been promised many offspring, but his wife, Sarah, was barren and old. So she decided she'd help God out of a jam. Sarah offered Hagar to her husband, and the girl became pregnant.

Now, things got tense around camp. The barren wife became more and more jealous of the pregnant servant. Finally Sarah mistreated Hagar so badly that she was forced to flee.

Hagar found herself on the desert road between Kadesh and Bered. She was utterly alone—no place to go. And she was pregnant. In that sandy wasteland, this poor girl had become a zero. She was a slave with no one to work for. A prospective mother with no family. An Egyptian in wild Canaan.

Finally, exhaustion broke through the emotions driving her on. Hagar stopped by a spring to rest. In this moment of total despair and isolation, someone called her by name: "Hagar, servant of Sarah."

Who knew her out there in that wasteland? And who cared? As it turned out, an angel of the Lord did. He asked where she was going. She replied, "I'm running . . ."

Then God, through this angel, gave Hagar the same kind of promise He'd given her master. He said, "I'll make your descendants too numerous to count." Her baby would be a boy, to be named Ishmael, meaning, "God hears."

So Hagar found the strength to survive. She returned to Abraham and Sarah, had her son, and became the mother of the Arab nations. This maidservant knew that God wasn't just up there in the stars over Abraham—He was down in the desert by her side. And she now called Him, "The God who sees me." She knew. He'd come close. He'd called her by name.

That's what makes the God of the Bible so special—particularly for lonely people. He calls us by name. He doesn't issue computer-generated form letters; He doesn't just shout from mountain tops. He calls out our name—even in the desert of isolation.

Breaking the Cycle of Loneliness

So this is the first thing you can do to break the cycle of loneliness. Listen, and then answer back. Start talking to the One who knows you intimately. If you're shy and introverted, that can become a strength. It can become a resource, not just a liability.

But you have to begin using that resource in the right way. Your introversion can't just go in circles—round and round inside you. That's a dead end. You need to open up the Word of God, look at the stories of Jesus, and start talking back. Opening up to God is the first step you can take toward opening up to life in general and other people in particular.

Lonely people often have a rather gloomy outlook

on life that shows in their social contacts. Warren Jones, a University of Tulsa psychologist, compared how groups of students dealt with new acquaintances during a fifteen-minute conversation. He divided the students into the lonely and the non-lonely.

Jones found that lonely students assumed that their new acquaintances didn't like them—even though that was rarely the case. And they didn't seem to like themselves much either. He also found that the lonely students were more negative in general than their counterparts.

Now we're getting to the heart of the matter. It's not just introversion that isolates people. It's negative introversion. Some individuals just haven't received a lot of positive input in their lives. Perhaps their childhood was painful. Perhaps they didn't receive the nurture that we all need.

When you haven't had a lot of positive stuff going in, it's hard to get positive stuff coming out. That's the dilemma of the chronically lonely. It can be a vicious circle. They usually haven't had warm relationships. That tends to isolate them. And the more isolated they are, the less likely they are to have warm relationships.

Is it possible to break the cycle? We've already said that personalities don't change much. Shy people don't become the life of the party.

Well, our tendency to be introverted may not disappear, but *negative* introversion can change. In other words, we may always be relatively quiet. But we don't always have to be gloomy and quiet.

Lonely No Longer 77

Finding the Nurture We Missed

Here's why. There's a wonderful source of positive input that's outside of us, separate from our family, separate from our acquaintances. We can receive the nurture that we missed, from the God who calls us by name.

Listen, God doesn't just call us by one name. He also gives us many other names. That's how He lavishes His grace on us. Listen to 1 John 3:1: "Behold what manner of love the Father has bestowed on us, that we should be called children of God!"

If you open up the New Testament and read any of the epistles, you will soon find yourself submerged in the wonderful names the heavenly Father gives His children.

Once we respond to the God who calls us by name and accept Him as Lord and Saviour, he can give us a new perspective.

Listen to how He labels believers: We're identified as children of God and assured that our citizenship is in heaven. We're God's chosen; He has anointed us, set His seal of ownership on us, and placed His own Spirit within us as a foretaste of future glories. We're vessels to be used for noble purposes, temples of God. The Father boasts about doing more than we can imagine through the power at work inside us.

This is the New Testament anthem which celebrates our identity, our names. Through image after image, God tries to make His perspective sink in. He wants us to understand exactly who we are *in* Christ. Listen to the apostle John's confident affirmation to believers: "And we know that the Son of God has come and has given us an understanding, that we may know Him who is true; and we are in Him who is true, in His Son Jesus Christ. This is the true God and eternal life." 1 John 5:20.

God will give us this understanding if we just let these New Testament names sink in—if we just accept by faith our identity in Christ. We need to know the One who is true, the One who is real, accepting the nourishment from His Word, face to face.

Lonely people desperately need this kind of positive nourishment in their lives. No one sets out to be lonely; no one plans to have an isolated life. People are simply shaped that way.

But we can reverse the cycle to a great extent. Our perspective won't change immediately. But if we just focus on what God is saying to us, if we just keep listening to the One who gives us all these beautiful names, that love will begin to sink in.

And then something wonderful happens. When you have a lot of wonderful names, you can pass along a few to others. When you're being affirmed and encouraged, you can afford to affirm others.

Lonely people miss so many opportunities. Meaningful human contact keeps sliding right by them. Why? Because they don't feel they have much to give. But when you've been touched by grace, you do have something to give. When God starts filling you up, you can afford to spill over a little bit.

University of California psychologist Karen Rook emphasizes this skill: matching the level of disclosure of your conversational partner. That is, we open up as the other person opens up. We respond to their personal information with our own personal information. In this way, we'll take advantage of those opportunities that seem to slip right by the lonely.

Please remember, the energy we need to start us moving out of our little circle of loneliness comes down to this: responding to the God who calls us by name. We've got to believe that He really is there, and we've got to start listening for that voice.

One summer night a Scottish youth named Peter decided to take a shortcut through the moors to a town named Bamburgh. The farther the lad walked, the darker the night became. The sky was starless and inky black. He could hear only the far-off bleating of sheep and the wind rustling.

Peter was very much alone out there amid the rock and heather, barely able to see two feet in front of him. His surroundings made it seem he was the only human being on the planet.

But suddenly a voice called out with great urgency, "Peter!"

The youth stopped, a bit unnerved. He called out into the dark, "Yes, who is it? What do you want?"

No response. Just a bit of wind over the deserted moorland. The lad concluded he'd been mistaken and walked on a few steps. Then he heard the voice again, more urgent than before: "Peter!"

He stopped in his tracks, bent forward to peer through the blackness, and stumbled to his knees. Reaching out a hand to the ground before him, he clutched thin air. The rock quarry! Sure enough, as

Peter carefully felt around in a semicircle, he discovered he'd stopped on the edge of an abandoned limestone quarry—one step from a fatal plunge into the deep.

Out there in the desolate moor, someone knew him, and someone cared. Peter Marshall never forgot that. Dedicating his life to the One who'd called him by name, he became one of America's outstanding preachers and chaplain to the United States Senate.

Have you been struggling with chronic loneliness? Are you feeling handicapped because you're shy and introverted? Begin using those qualities for something positive. Use them to get to know the God who calls you by name intimately. You will find that even loneliness can be enriching if it chases you to God, clears your heart, and lets your very best part shine through.